·DAN COATE꙳

Easy Piano
Collection

Pop, Country,
Movie & TV Hits

Alfred

Alfred Music
P.O. Box 10003
Van Nuys, CA 91410-0003
alfred.com

ISBN-10: 1-57623-535-1
ISBN-13: 978-1-57623-535-5

ALPHABETICAL INDEX

ALPHABETICAL INDEX

CONTENTS BY CATEGORY

POPULAR FAVORITES

COUNTRY HITS

MOVIE HITS

TV THEMES

YOU'LL SEE

Words and Music by
MADONNA CICCONE and
DAVID FOSTER
Arranged by DAN COATES

You'll See - 4 - 1

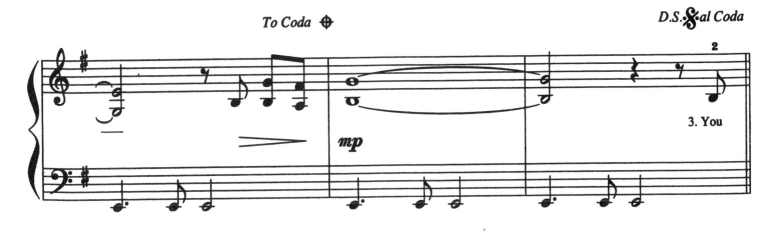

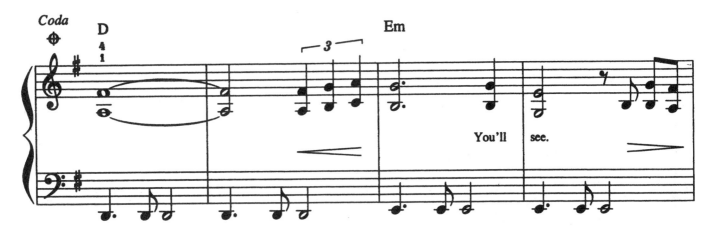

Verse 2:
You think that I can never laugh again,
You'll see.
You think that you've destroyed my faith in love.
You think after all you've done,
I'll never find my way back home.
You'll see, somehow, some day.   *(To Chorus:)*

Verse 3:
You think that you are strong, but you are weak,
You'll see.
It takes more strength to cry, admit defeat.
I have truth on my side,
You only have deceit.
You'll see, somehow, some day.   *(To Chorus:)*

ALWAYS AND FOREVER

Words and Music by
ROD TEMPERTON
Arranged by DAN COATES

ANGEL EYES

Composed by
JIM BRICKMAN
Arranged by DAN COATES

Angel Eyes - 3 - 1

Angel Eyes - 3 - 3

BECAUSE YOU LOVED ME
(Theme from "Up Close & Personal")

Words and Music by
DIANE WARREN
Arranged by DAN COATES

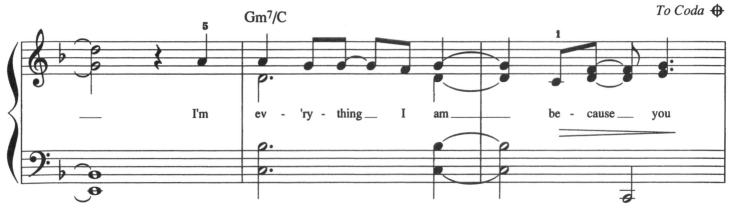

COUNT ON ME

Words and Music by
BABYFACE, WHITNEY HOUSTON
and MICHAEL HOUSTON
Arranged by DAN COATES

Count on Me - 5 - 1

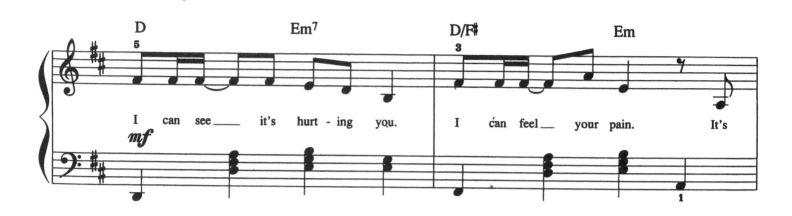

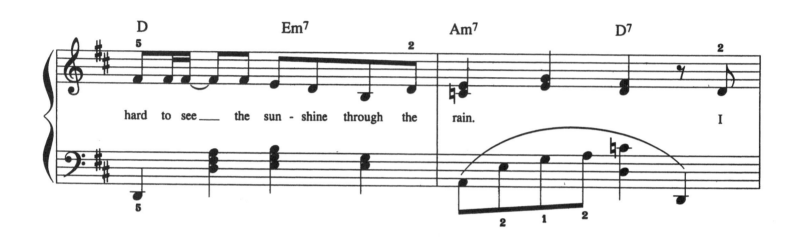

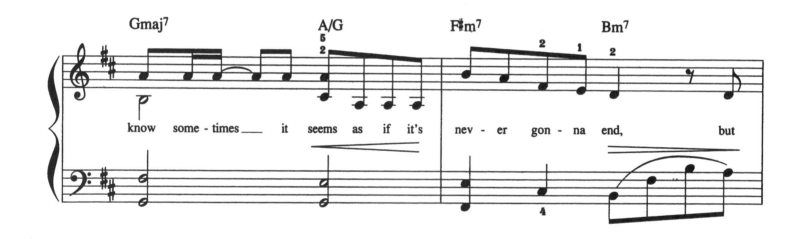

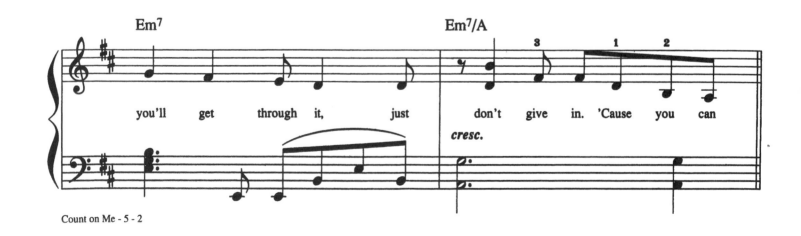

D.S. %al Coda I

Coda I

me.
mp
know some - times ___ it seems as if we're stand - in' all a - lone. But
mf
we'll get through it, 'cause love won't let us fold.
cresc.
count on. ___ There's a place in - side of all of us where our
mf

DESPERADO

Words and Music by
DON HENLEY and GLENN FREY
Arranged by DAN COATES

Slowly

Des-per - a - do, why don't you come to your sens - es?__ You been
- a - do, oh, you ain't get-tin' no young-er,__ your

out rid - in' fenc - es for so long now.__ Oh, you're a
pain and your hun - ger they're driv - ing you home.__ And

hard one, I know that you got your rea - sons, these
free-dom, well, that's just some peo-ple talk - in', your

things that are pleas - in' you can hurt you some - how.__
pris - on is walk - in' through this world all a - lone.__

Desperado - 3 - 1

27

Desperado - 3 - 2

From the Motion Picture "ROBIN HOOD: PRINCE OF THIEVES"

(EVERYTHING I DO) I DO IT FOR YOU

Words and Music by
BRYAN ADAMS, ROBERT JOHN LANGE
and **MICHAEL KAMEN**
Arranged by DAN COATES

(Everything I Do) I Do It for You - 5 - 1

DREAMING OF YOU

Words and Music by
TOM SNOW and
FRAN GOLDE
Arranged by DAN COATES

Dreaming of You - 4 - 1

EXHALE
(Shoop Shoop)

Words and Music by
BABYFACE
Arranged by DAN COATES

Exhale - 4 - 1

FROM A DISTANCE

Lyrics and Music by
JULIE GOLD
Arranged by DAN COATES

Verse 2:
From a distance, we all have enough
And no one is in need.
There are no guns, no bombs, no diseases,
No hungry mouths to feed.
From a distance, we are instruments
Marching in a common band;
Playing songs of hope, playing songs of peace,
They're the songs of every man.

Verse 3:
From a distance, you look like my friend
Even though we are at war.
From a distance, I just cannot comprehend
What all this fighting is for.
From a distance, there is harmony
And it echoes through the land.
It's the hope of hopes. It's the love of loves.
It's the heart of every man.

THE GREATEST LOVE OF ALL

Words by
LINDA CREED

Music by
MICHAEL MASSER
Arranged by DAN COATES

The Greatest Love of All - 4 - 1

From the Original Motion Picture Soundtrack "DON JUAN DeMARCO"

HAVE YOU EVER REALLY LOVED A WOMAN?

Lyrics by
BRYAN ADAMS and ROBERT JOHN "MUTT" LANGE

Music by
MICHAEL KAMEN
Arranged by DAN COATES

Have You Ever Really Loved a Woman? - 4 - 1

From the Motion Picture "THE WOMAN IN RED"

I JUST CALLED TO SAY I LOVE YOU

Words and Music by
STEVIE WONDER
Arranged by DAN COATES

I Just Called to Say I Love You - 3 - 1

I Just Called to Say I Love You - 3 - 2

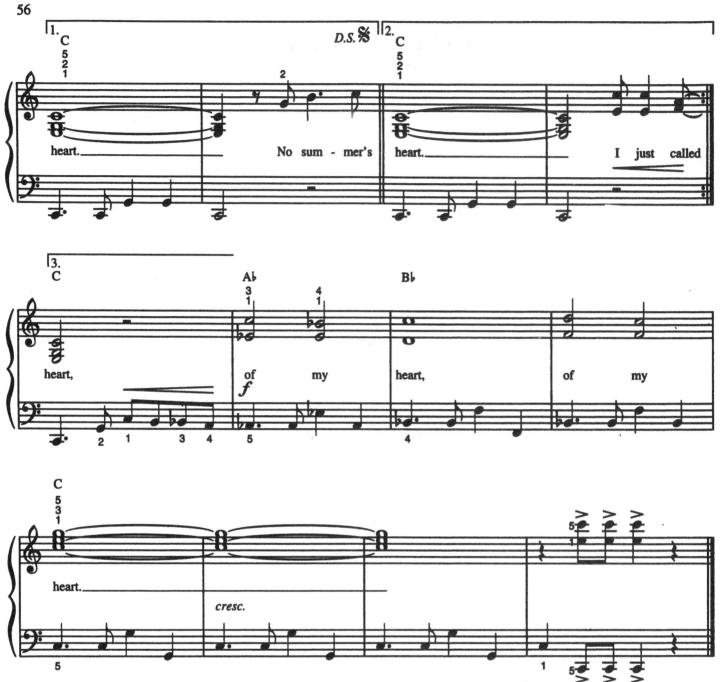

Verse 3:
No summer's high; no warm July;
No harvest moon to light one tender August night.
No autumn breeze; no falling leaves;
Not even time for birds to fly to southern skies.

Verse 4:
No Libra sun; no Halloween;
No giving thanks to all the Christmas joy you bring.
But what it is, though old so new
To fill your heart like no three words could ever do.
(To Chorus:)

I'D LIE FOR YOU
(And That's the Truth)

Words and Music by
DIANNE WARREN
Arranged by DAN COATES

I'd Lie for You - 5 - 1

MORE THAN WORDS

Lyrics and Music by
BETTENCOURT, CHERONE
Arranged by DAN COATES

Moderate rock ballad ♩ = 92

More Than Words - 5 - 1

64

More Than Words - 5 - 3

Verse 2:
Now that I have tried to talk to you
And make you understand,
All you have to do is close your eyes
And just reach out your hands
And touch me, hold me close, don't ever let me go.
More than words is all I ever needed you to show.
Then you wouldn't have to say
That you love me, 'cause I'd already know.

OPEN ARMS

Words and Music by
STEVE PERRY and
JOHNATHAN CAIN
Arranged by DAN COATES

Open Arms - 3 - 1

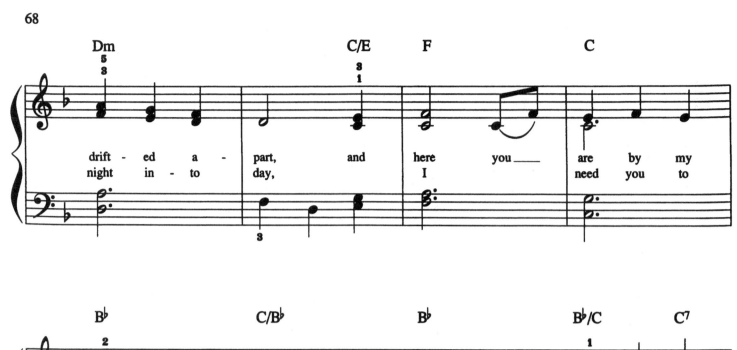

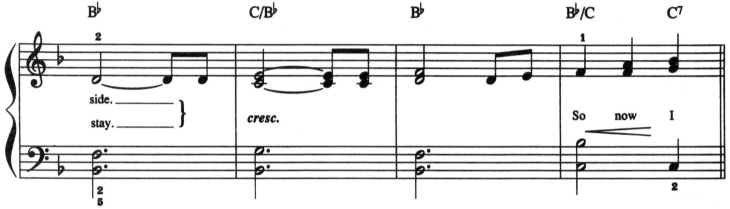

ONE OF US

Words and Music by
ERIC BAZILIAN
Arranged by DAN COATES

God had a name, ___ what would it be and would you call it to his face,
God had a face, ___ what would it look like and would you want to see,

One of Us - 4 - 1

One of Us - 4 - 2

REACH

Words and Music by
GLORIA ESTEFAN and
DIANE WARREN
Arranged by DAN COATES

1. Some dreams ____ live on in time ____ for - ev - er.
2. Some days ____ are meant to be ____ re - mem - bered.

Those dreams ____ you want with all ____ your
Those days, ____ we rise a - bove ____ the

heart. ____
stars. ____

And I'll
So, I'll

From the Twentieth Century-Fox Motion Picture "THE ROSE"

THE ROSE

Words and Music by
AMANDA McBROOM
Arranged by DAN COATES

The Rose - 3 - 1

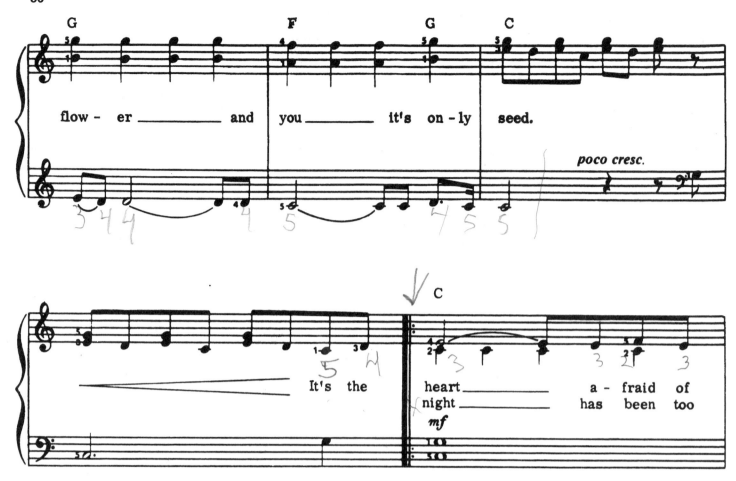

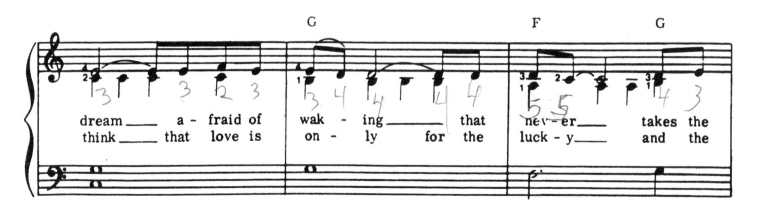

STAIRWAY TO HEAVEN

Words and Music by
JIMMY PAGE and ROBERT PLANT
Arranged by DAN COATES

83

Stairway to Heaven - 5 - 2

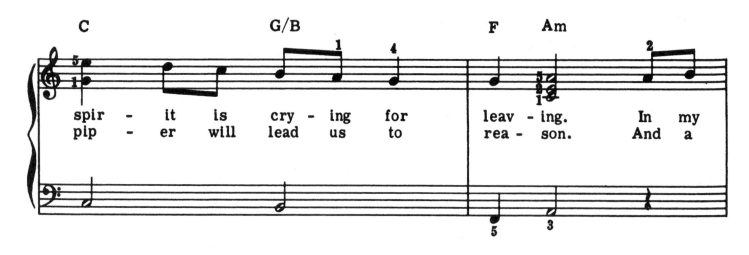

spir - it is cry - ing for leav - ing. In my
pip - er will lead us to rea - son. And a

thoughts I have seen___ rings of smoke through the trees,___ and the
new day will dawn___ for those who stand long,___ and the

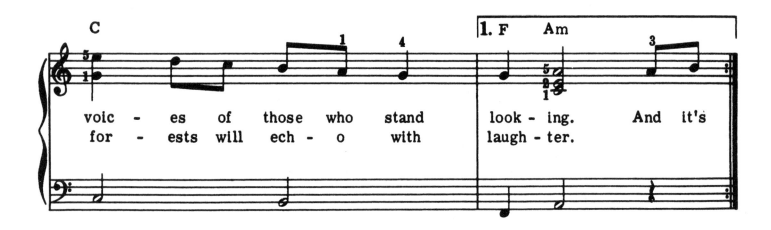

voic - es of those who stand look - ing. And it's
for - ests will ech - o with laugh - ter.

1. F   Am

2. F   Am

laugh - ter.

With a strong beat

If there's a bus - tle in your
Your head is hum - ming and it

Stairway to Heaven - 5 - 4

THE SWEETEST DAYS

Words and Music by
WENDY WALDMAN, JON LIND
and PHIL GALDSTON
Arranged by DAN COATES

The Sweetest Days - 3 - 3

TEARS IN HEAVEN

Words and Music by
WILL JENNINGS and ERIC CLAPTON
Arranged by DAN COATES

Tears in Heaven - 4 - 1

ALWAYS

Written by
JONATHAN LEWIS, WAYNE LEWIS
and DAVID LEWIS
Arranged by DAN COATES

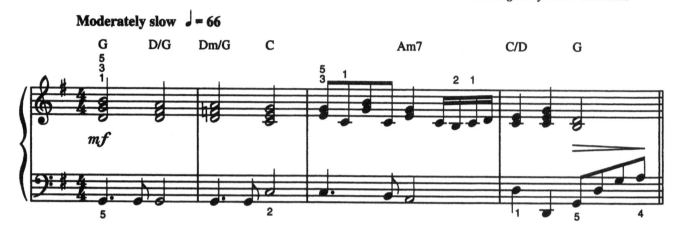

1. Girl, you are to me all _____ that a wo-man should be, and I
2. Come with me, my sweet; let's go make a fam - i - ly. And

ded - i - cate my life to you al - ways. A love like yours is rare; it
they will bring us joy for al - ways. Oh, boy, I love you so; I can't

must have been sent from up a - bove. _ And I
find e - nough ways to let you know. _ But you

know you'll stay this way for al - ways. And
can be sure I'm yours for al - ways. And

we both know that our love will grow. And for -

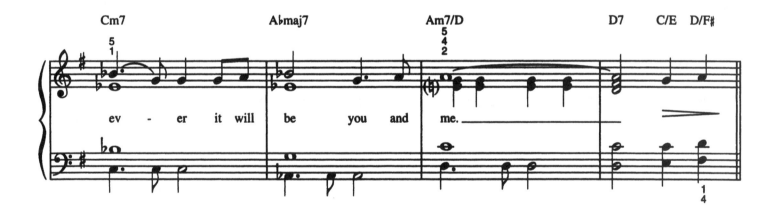

ev - er it will be you and me. _

Chorus:

Ooh, you're like the sun, chas-ing all the _ rain a-way. _ When you come a-round, you bring

Always - 3 - 2

bright - er days. You're the pe - rfect one, for me,___ and you for-ev-er will be. And

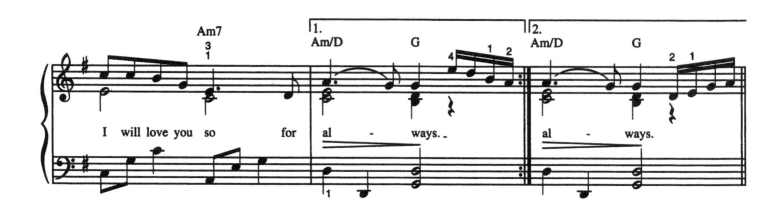

I will love you so for al - ways.___ al - ways.

Ooh ___ ooh - hoo. I will love you so for al - ways.

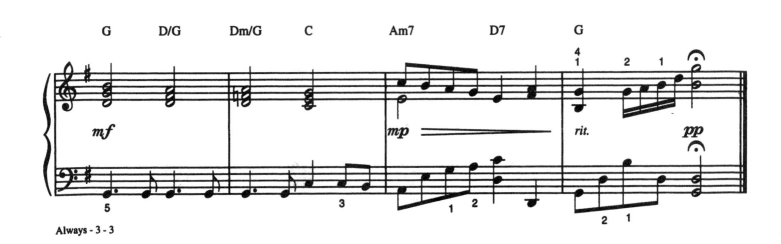

Always - 3 - 3

From the Original Motion Picture Soundtrack ''BEACHES''

THE WIND BENEATH MY WINGS

Words and Music by
LARRY HENLEY and JEFF SILBAR
Arranged by DAN COATES

The Wind Beneath My Wings - 5 - 1

3. It might have appeared to go unnoticed
   that I've got it all here in my heart.
   I want you to know I know the truth:
   I would be nothing without you.

YOU ARE NOT ALONE

Written and Composed by
R. KELLY
Arranged by DAN COATES

You Are Not Alone - 5 - 4

ANGELS AMONG US

Words and Music by
BECKY HOBBS and DON GOODMAN
Arranged by DAN COATES

Spoken: I was walking home from school on a cold winter day, took a short cut through the woods and I lost my way. It was getting late and I was scared and alone, then a kind old man took my hand and led me home. Sung: Ma - ma could - n't see him, but

Angels Among Us - 3 - 1

Additional lyrics

Spoken: *When life held troubled times and had me down on my knees*
There's always been someone to come along and comfort me.
A kind word from a stranger, to lend a helping hand,
A phone call from a friend just to say I understand.
Sung: *Now, ain't it kind of funny, at the dark end of the road,*
Someone lights the way with just a single ray of hope.
(To Chorus)

YOUR CHEATIN' HEART

Words and Music by
HANK WILLIAMS
Arranged by DAN COATES

THE DANCE

Words and Music by
TONY ARATA
Arranged by DAN COATES

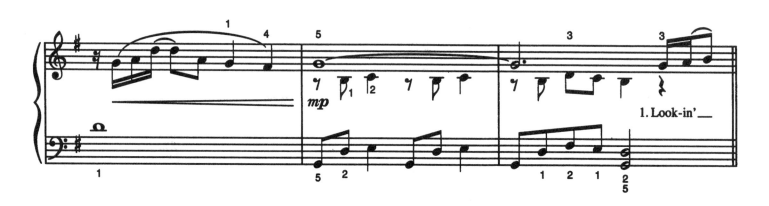

1. Look-in' __

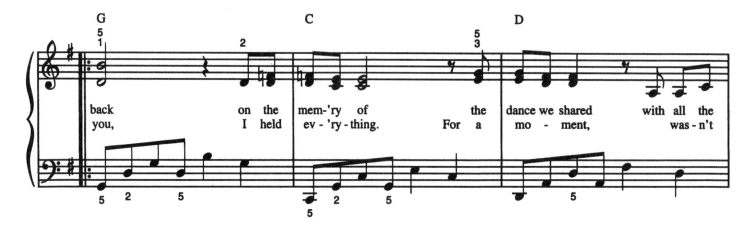

back   on the   mem-'ry of   the   dance we shared   with all the
you,   I held   ev-'ry-thing.   For a   mo - ment,   was-n't

stars a - bove.   For a   mo - ment,   all the   world was right.   How could
I the king?   If I'd   on-ly known   how the   king would fall.   Hey,

The Dance - 3 - 1

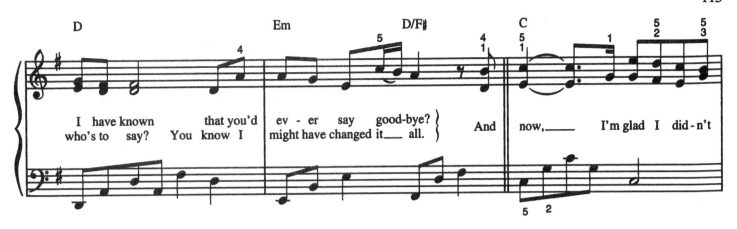

I have known   that you'd   ev - er   say   good-bye?
who's to   say?   You   know I   might have changed it___ all.   And   now,___   I'm glad I   did-n't

know___   the way it   all would   end,___   the way   it   all would   go.___   Our

lives___   are bet - ter   left to   chance.___   I could have missed the   pain,___   but I'd have had to

miss   the___   dance.___   *mp*   2. Hold - ing

dance.   Yes, my   life,_____   it's bet - ter left to   chance._____   I could have missed the

pain,_____   but I'd have had to   miss   the_____   dance.

decresc.   *mp*   *rit.*

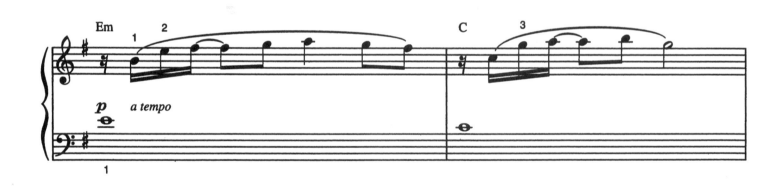

p   *a tempo*

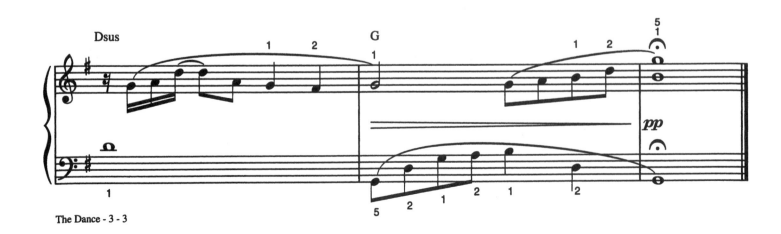

pp

I CAN'T STOP LOVING YOU

Words and Music by
DON GIBSON
Arranged by DAN COATES

I Can't Stop Loving You - 3 - 1

I Can't Stop Loving You - 3 - 2

GO REST HIGH ON THAT MOUNTAIN

Words and Music by
VINCE GILL
Arranged by DAN COATES

Slowly, in Gospel style

I CAN LOVE YOU LIKE THAT

Words and Music by
STEVE DIAMOND, MARIBETH DERRY
and JENNIFER KIMBALL
Arranged by DAN COATES

From the Warner Bros. Film "PURE COUNTRY"

I CROSS MY HEART

Words and Music by
STEVE DORFF and ERIC KAZ
Arranged by DAN COATES

I Cross My Heart - 5 - 1

126

I Cross My Heart - 5 - 4

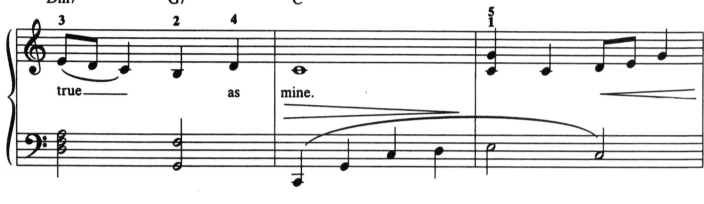

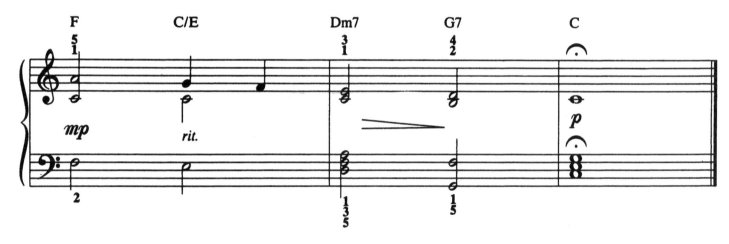

Additional Lyrics

2. You will always be the miracle
   That makes my life complete.
   And as long as there's a breath in me
   I'll make yours just as sweet.
   As we look into the future,
   It's as far as we can see.
   So let's make each tomorrow
   Be the best that it can be.
   (To Chorus)

From the Motion Picture "THE BODYGUARD"

I WILL ALWAYS LOVE YOU

Words and Music by
DOLLY PARTON
Arranged by DAN COATES

I Will Always Love You - 3 - 1

I Will Always Love You - 3 - 2

Extra Lyrics:

3. I hope life treats you kind
   And I hope you have all you've dreamed of.
   I wish you joy and happiness.
   But above all this,
   I wish you love.

I LOVE THE WAY YOU LOVE ME

Words and Music by
VICTORIA SHAW and CHUCK CANNON
Arranged by DAN COATES

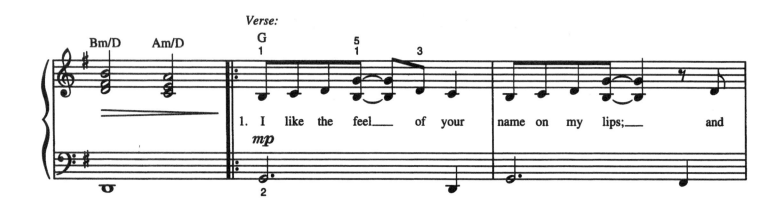

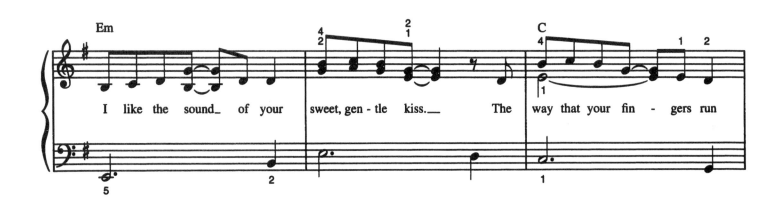

I Love the Way You Love Me - 4 - 1

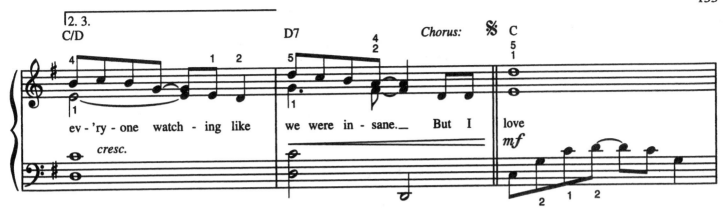

ev - 'ry - one watch - ing like we were in - sane.__ But I love

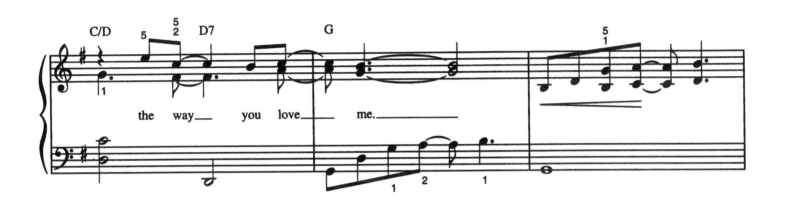

the way__ you love__ me.__

Strong and wild,__ slow and eas - y, heart and soul,__

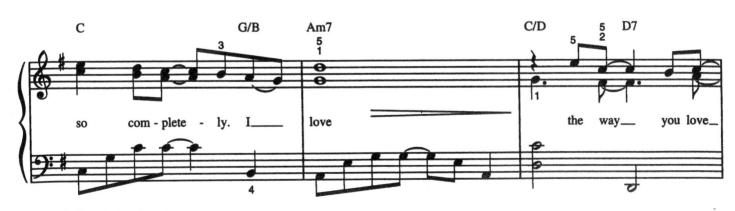

so com - plete - ly. I__ love the way__ you love__

I Love the Way You Love Me - 4 - 2

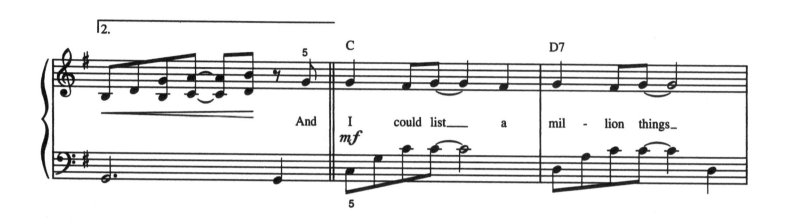

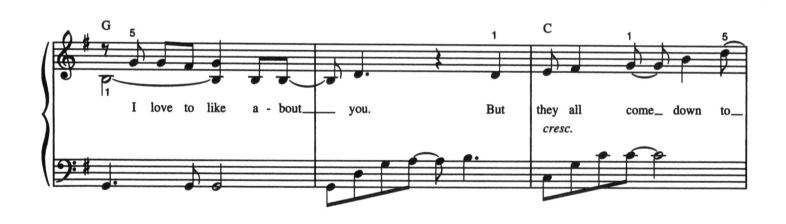

I Love the Way You Love Me - 4 - 3

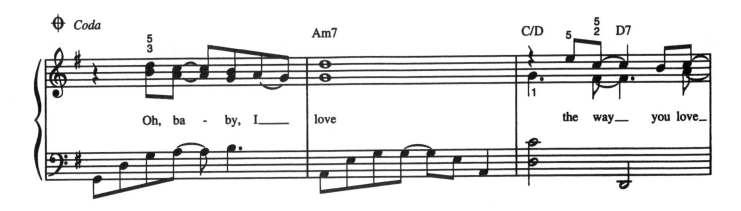

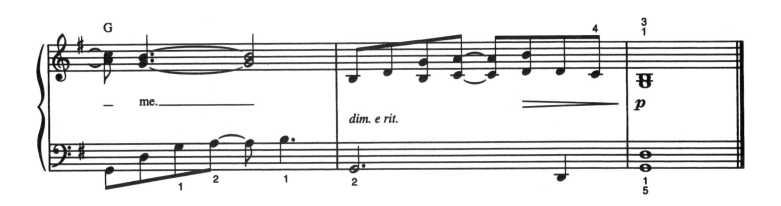

Verse 2:
I like the way your eyes dance when you laugh
And how you enjoy your two hour bath.
And how you convinced me to dance in the rain
With everyone watching like we were insane.
(To Chorus:)

Verse 3:
I like to imitate ol' Jerry Lee
While you roll your eyes when I'm slightly off key.
And I like the innocent way that you cry
At sappy old movies you've seen hundreds of times.
(To Chorus:)

I SWEAR

Words and Music by
GARY BAKER and FRANK MYERS
Arranged by DAN COATES

I see the ques - tion in___ your eyes,___
I'll give you ev - 'ry - thing__ I can,___

__ I know what's weigh - ing on__ your mind,___ but you can be sure___
__ I'll build your dreams__ with these_ two hands,___ and we'll hang some mem-

I Swear - 4 - 1

I Swear - 4 - 2

IF TOMORROW NEVER COMES

Words and Music by
KENT BLAZY and GARTH BROOKS
Arranged by DAN COATES

Verse 2:
'Cause I've lost loved ones in my life
Who never knew how much I loved them.
Now I live with the regret
That my true feelings for them never were revealed.
So I made a promise to myself
To say each day how much she means to me
And avoid the circumstance
Where there's no second chance
To tell her how I feel. 'Cause... *(To Chorus:)*

IN THIS LIFE

Words and Music by
MIKE REID and
ALLEN SHAMBLIN
Arranged by DAN COATES

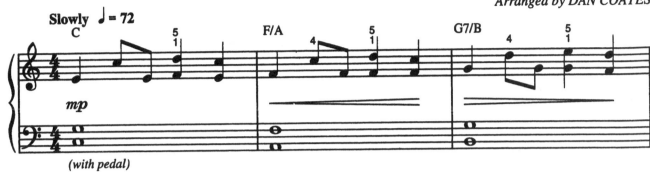

For all I'd been blessed with in my life,

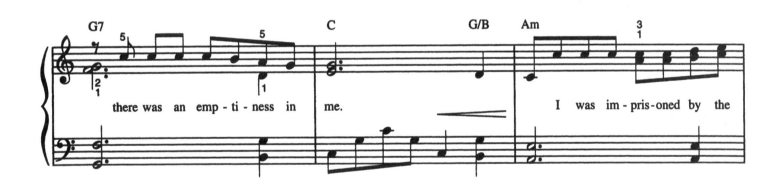

there was an emp-ti-ness in me. I was im-pris-oned by the

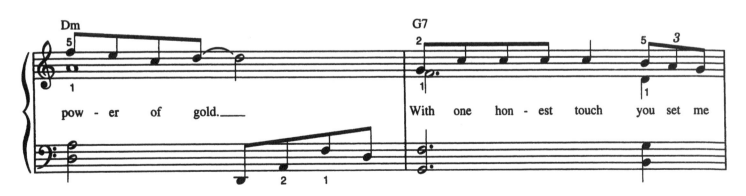

pow - er of gold. With one hon-est touch you set me

In This Life - 3 - 1

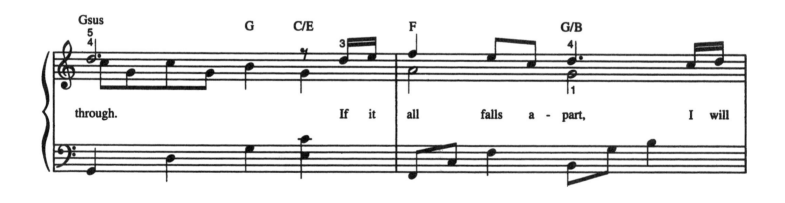

true;   in this   life   I   was   loved___   by   you.

you.   In this   life   I   was

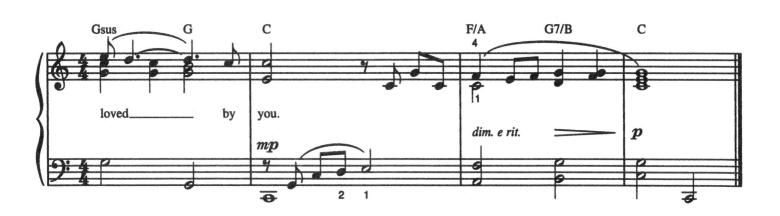

loved_____   by   you.

dim. e rit.

Verse 2:
For every mountain I have climbed,
Every raging river crossed,
You were the treasure that I longed to find.
Without your love I would be lost.
(To Chorus:)

In This Life - 3 - 3

THE KEEPER OF THE STARS

Words and Music by
KAREN STALEY, DANNY MAYO and DICKEY LEE
Arranged by DAN COATES

The Keeper of the Stars - 4 - 1

ONE FRIEND

Words and Music by
DAN SEALS
Arranged by DAN COATES

One Friend - 3 - 1

SINGING THE BLUES

Words and Music by
MELVIN ENDSLEY
Arranged by DAN COATES

Singing the Blues - 3 - 1

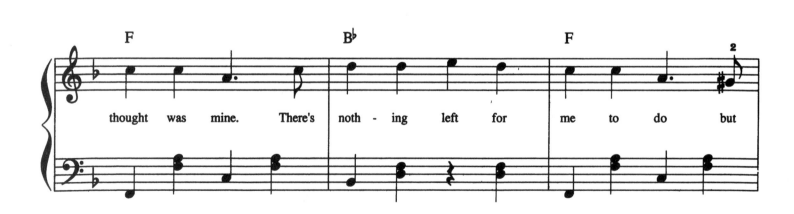

cry _____ o - ver you.__ Well, I nev - er felt more like

run - ning a - way,___ but why should I go___ 'cause I could - n't stay___ with -

out you. You got me sing - ing the blues.

Well, I blues.

THE RIVER

Words and Music by
VICTORIA SHAW and GARTH BROOKS
Arranged by DAN COATES

The River - 4 - 1

Good Lord as ___ my cap - tain, ___ I can make it through ___ them all. ___ Yes, I will

Coda ⊕

Yes, I will sail my ves - sel ___ 'til the

riv - er runs ___ dry. ___

Verse 2:
Too many times we stand aside
And let the waters slip away
'Til what we put off 'til tomorrow
Has now become today.
So, don't you sit upon the shoreline
And say you're satisfied.
Choose to chance the rapids
And dare to dance the tide.
Yes, I will... *(To Chorus:)*

A THOUSAND MILES FROM NOWHERE

Words and Music by
DWIGHT YOAKAM
Arranged by DAN COATES

Moderate, steady tempo

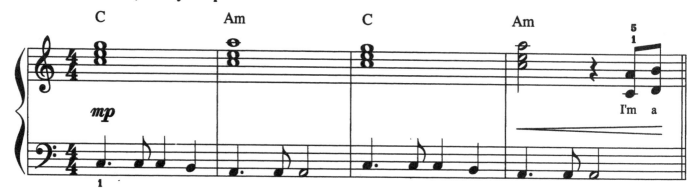

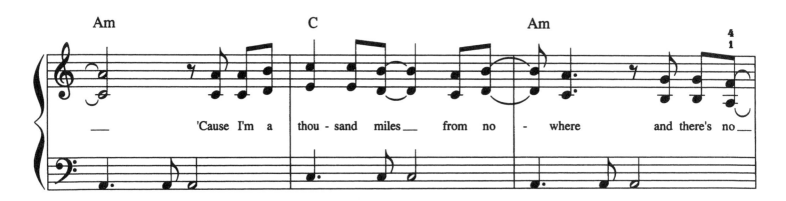

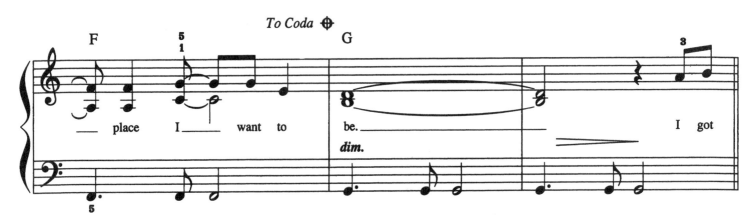

A Thousand Miles from Nowhere - 2 - 2

TO ME

Words and Music by
MACK DAVID and
MIKE REID
Arranged by DAN COATES

Slowly and expressively

To Me - 3 - 1

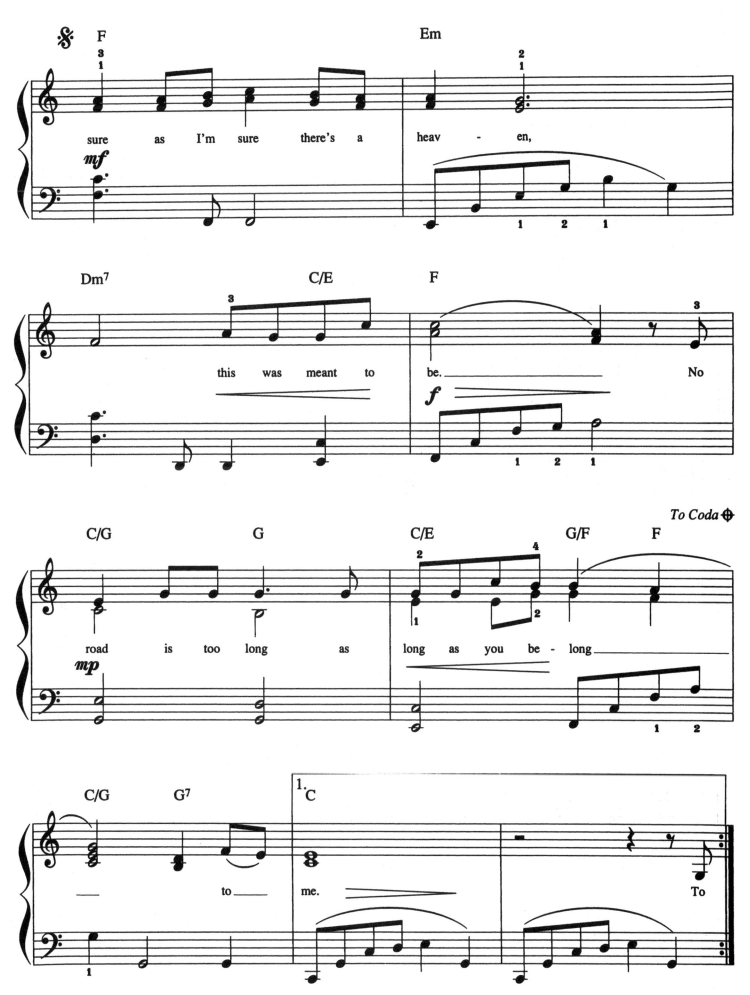

THE VOWS GO UNBROKEN
(Always True to You)

Words and Music by
GARY BURR and ERIC KAZ
Arranged by DAN COATES

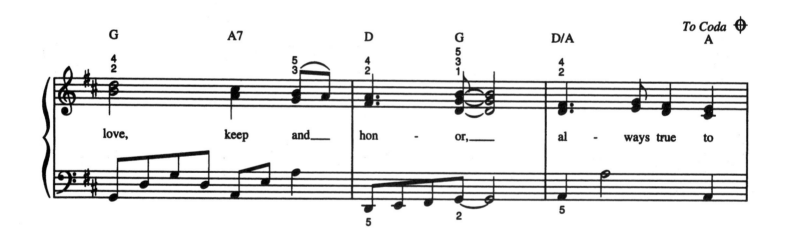

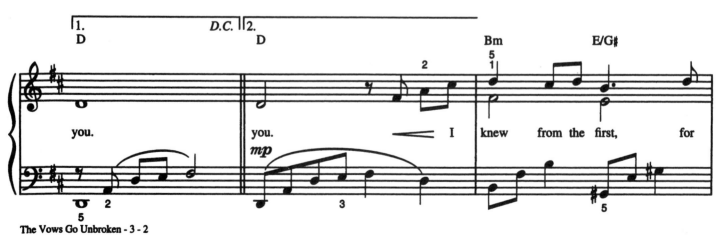

The Vows Go Unbroken - 3 - 2

Verse 3:
Though I have been tempted,
Oh I have never strayed.
I'd die before I'd damage
This union we have made. *(To Chorus:)*

UNANSWERED PRAYERS

Words and Music by
LARRY B. BASTIAN, PAT ALGER
and GARTH BROOKS
Arranged by DAN COATES

Slowly ♩ = 66

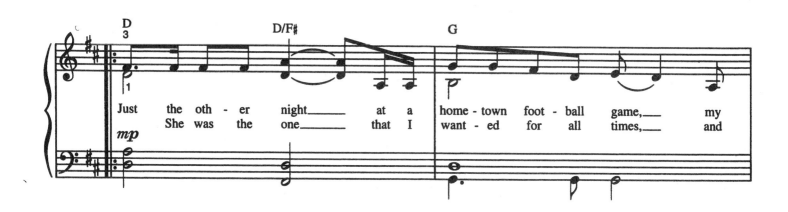

Just the oth-er night____ at a home-town foot-ball game,____ my
She was the one____ that I want-ed for all times,____ and

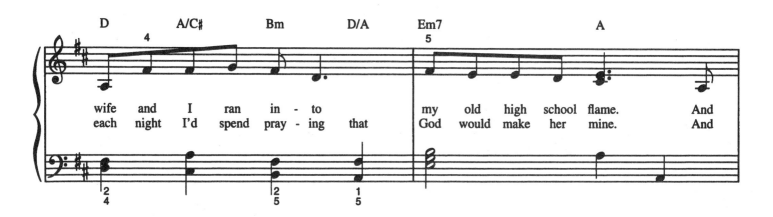

wife and I ran in-to my old high school flame. And
each night I'd spend pray-ing that God would make her mine. And

as I in-tro-duced them, the past came back to me, and I
if He'd on-ly grant me this wish I'd wished back then, I'd

Unanswered Prayers - 4 - 1

are un-an-swered___ prayers.

She was-n't quite the an-gel that I re-mem-bered in my dreams, and I could

tell that time had changed me in her eyes too, it seemed. We tried to

talk a-bout the old days, there was-n't much we could re-call. I guess the

Lord knows what He's do-ing af-ter all.___ And

YOUR LOVE AMAZES ME

Words and Music by
CHUCK JONES and AMANDA HUNT
Arranged by DAN COATES

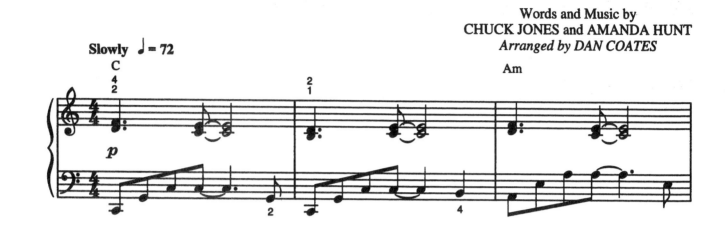

1. I've seen the sev-en won-ders

of the world.__ I've seen the beau-ty of dia-monds and pearls.__

Your Love Amazes Me - 4 - 1

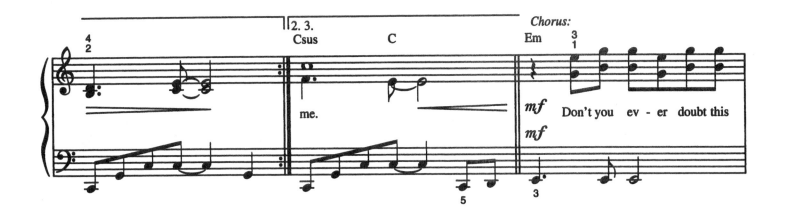

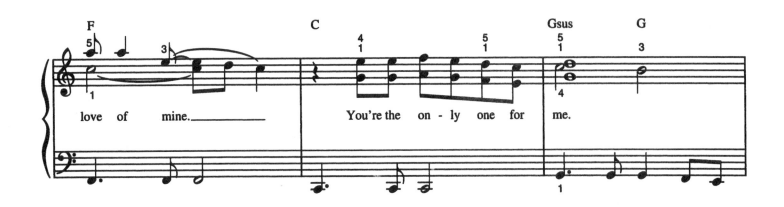

Your Love Amazes Me - 4 - 2

For - ev - er faith - ful - ly, your love a - maz - es me.

Your love, your love,___

your love a - maz - es me.

Your Love Amazes Me - 4 - 3

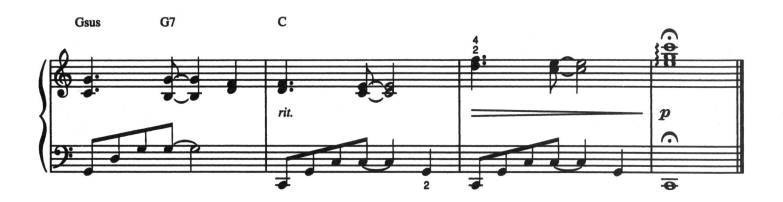

Verse 2:
I've seen a sunset that would make you cry,
And colors of a rainbow reaching 'cross the sky.
The moon in all its phases, but
Your love amazes me.
(To Chorus:)

Verse 3:
I've prayed for miracles that never came.
I got down on my knees in the pouring rain.
But only you could save me,
Your love amazes me.
(To Chorus:)

From the Soundtrack of PBS Series "The CIVIL WAR" a Film by Ken Burns

ASHOKAN FAREWELL

By JAY UNGAR
Arranged by DAN COATES

Ashokan Farewell - 4 - 1

Ashokan Farewell - 4 - 2

Ashokan Farewell - 4 - 3

Ashokan Farewell - 4 - 4

Theme from the TV Series "CHICAGO HOPE"

Theme from CHICAGO HOPE

Music by
MARK ISHAM
Arranged by DAN COATES

Theme from Chicago Hope - 2 - 2

BEVERLY HILLS, 90210
(Main Theme)

By JOHN E. DAVIS
Arranged by DAN COATES

Moderate rock beat

Beverly Hills, 90210 - 2 - 1

Beverly Hills, 90210 - 2 - 2

I'LL BE THERE FOR YOU
(Theme from ''Friends'')

Words by
DAVID CRANE, MARTA KAUFFMAN, ALLEE WILLIS,
PHIL SOLEM and DANNY WILDE

Music by
MICHAEL SKLOFF
Arranged by DAN COATES

Fast rock ♩ = 176

1. So, no ___ one told you life ___ was gon - na be ___ this way.
2. You're still ___ in bed at ten ___ and work be - gan ___ at eight.

Your job's ___ a joke, you're broke, ___ your love life's D. O. A.
You've burned ___ your break - fast, so ___ far, ev - 'ry - thing is great.

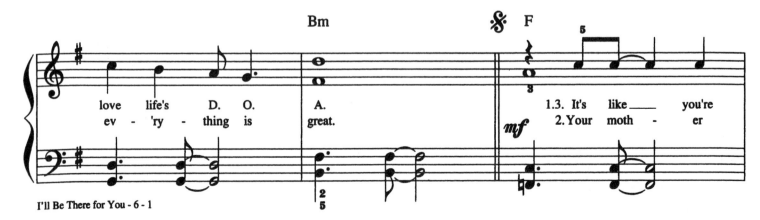

O. A.
thing is great.

1.3. It's like ___ you're
2.Your moth - er

I'll Be There for You - 6 - 1

From the TV Show "JEOPARDY"

JEOPARDY THEME

Music by
MERV GRIFFIN
Arranged by DAN COATES

Jeopardy Theme - 2 - 1

Jeopardy Theme - 2 - 2

Theme from the TV Series "L.A. LAW"

L.A. LAW
Main Title

By
MIKE POST
Arranged by DAN COATES

L.A. Law - 2 - 1

L.A. Law - 2 - 2

LINUS AND LUCY

By VINCE GUARALDI
Arranged by DAN COATES

Brightly, with spirit ♩ = 132

Linus and Lucy - 2 - 1

Linus and Lucy - 2 - 2

Theme from the PBS Series "MASTERPIECE THEATRE"

THE MASTERPIECE

By J.J. MOURET
and PAUL PARNES
Arranged by DAN COATES

The Masterpiece - 2 - 1

The Masterpiece - 2 - 2

Theme Song from the Mirisch-G&E Production, "THE PINK PANTHER," a United Artists Release

THE PINK PANTHER

Music by
HENRY MANCINI
Arranged by DAN COATES

The Pink Panther - 2 - 1

The Pink Panther - 2 - 2

SONG FROM "M*A*S*H"
(Suicide Is Painless)

Words and Music by
MIKE ALTMAN and JOHNNY MANDEL
Arranged by DAN COATES

Song from "M*A*S*H" - 2 - 1

1. Try to find a way to make
   All our little joys relate
   Without that ever-present hate
   But now I know that it's too late.
   And -(Chorus)

3. The game of life is hard to play,
   I'm going to lose it anyway,
   The losing card I'll someday lay,
   So this is all I have to say,
   That -(Chorus)

4. The only way to win, is cheat
   And lay it down before I'm beat,
   And to another give a seat
   For that's the only painless feat.
   'Cause: -(Chorus)

5. The sword of time will pierce our skins,
   It doesn't hurt when it begins
   But as it works its way on in,
   The pain grows stronger, watch it grin.
   For: -(Chorus)

6. A brave man once requested me
   To answer questions that are key,
   Is it to be or not to be
   And I replied; "Oh, why ask me."
   'Cause: -(Chorus)

Song from "M*A*S*H" - 2 - 2

THANK GOD FOR A FRIEND LIKE YOU
(Main Title from "Hope & Gloria")

Words by
CHERI STEINKELLNER

Music by
CRAIG SAFAN
Arranged by DAN COATES

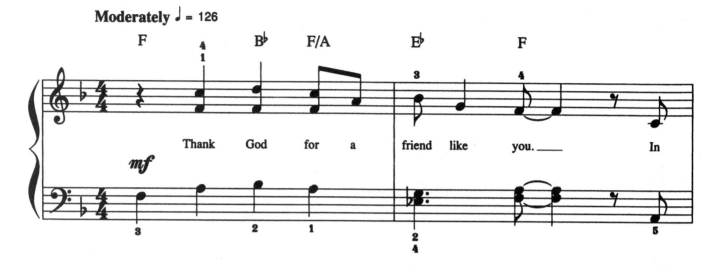

Thank God for a Friend Like You - 2 - 1

THEME FROM MURDER ONE

Music by
MIKE POST
Arranged by DAN COATES

Theme from Murder One - 2 - 1

Theme from Murder One - 2 - 2

Theme from "PICKET FENCES"

By STEWART LEVIN
Arranged by DAN COATES

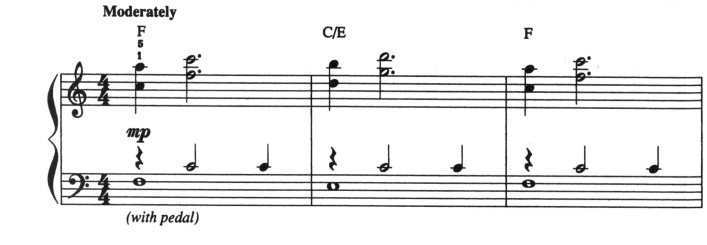

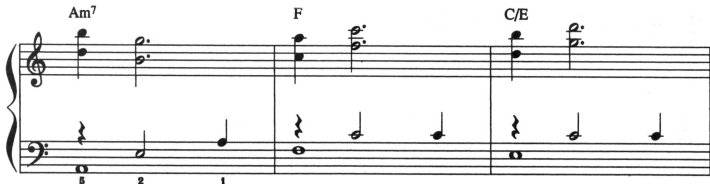

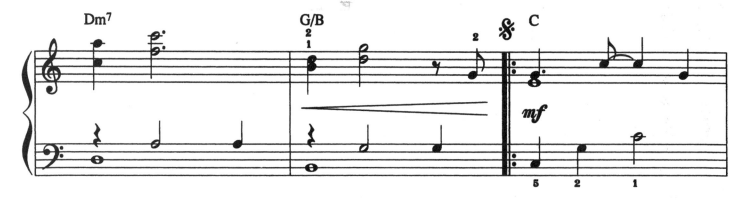

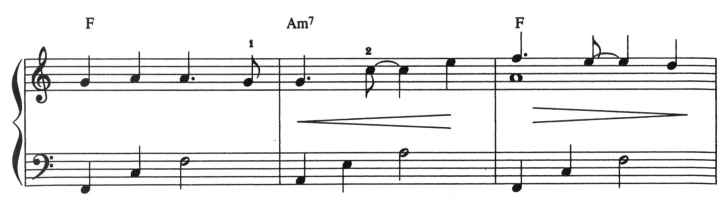

Theme from "Picket Fences" - 2 - 1

THEME FROM "THE SIMPSONS"

Music by
DANNY ELFMAN
Arranged by DAN COATES

Moderately Fast (♩ = 168)

The Simp - sons!

Theme from "The Simpsons" - 4 - 1

Theme from "The Simpsons" - 4 - 2

Theme from "The Simpsons" - 4 - 3

Theme from "The Simpsons" - 4 - 4

THEME FROM INSPECTOR GADGET

Words and Music by
HAIM SABAN and SHUKI LEVY
Arranged by DAN COATES

Theme from Inspector Gadget - 4 - 1

"In - spec - tor Gad - et."

"In - spec - tor Gad - get."

No chord

Theme from Inspector Gadget - 4 - 2

214

Theme from the TV Series "MARRIED . . . WITH CHILDREN"

LOVE AND MARRIAGE

Words by
SAMMY CAHN

Music by
JAMES VAN HEUSEN
Arranged by DAN COATES

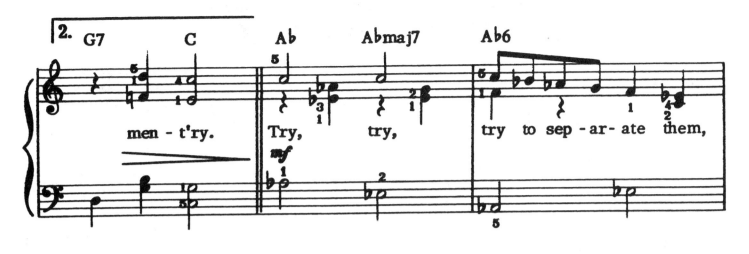

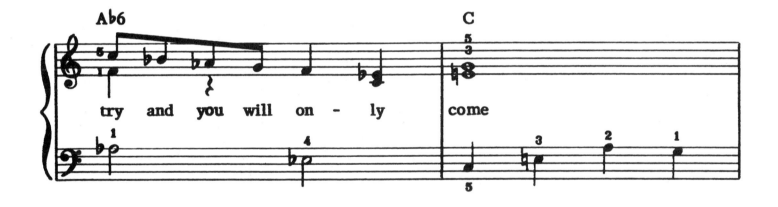

Love and Marriage - 3 - 2

go to - geth - er like a   horse and car - riage.

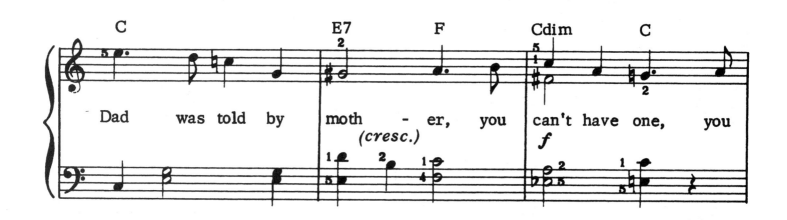

Dad   was told by   moth - er, you   can't have one,   you

(cresc.)

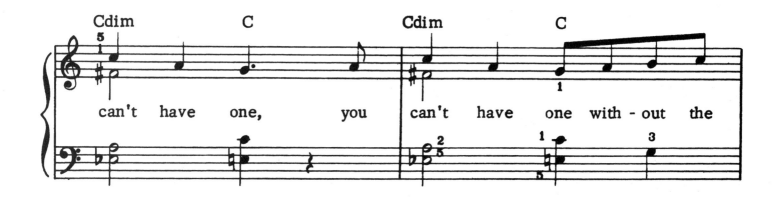

can't have one,   you   can't have   one with - out the

oth -   er!

Paramount Pictures Presents a Lorimar-Martin Elfand Production-
a Taylor Hackford Film "AN OFFICER AND A GENTLEMAN"

UP WHERE WE BELONG

Words by
WILL JENNINGS

By
WILL JENNINGS, BUFFY SAINTE-MARIE
and JACK NITZSCHE
Arranged by DAN COATES

Up Where We Belong - 5 - 1

220

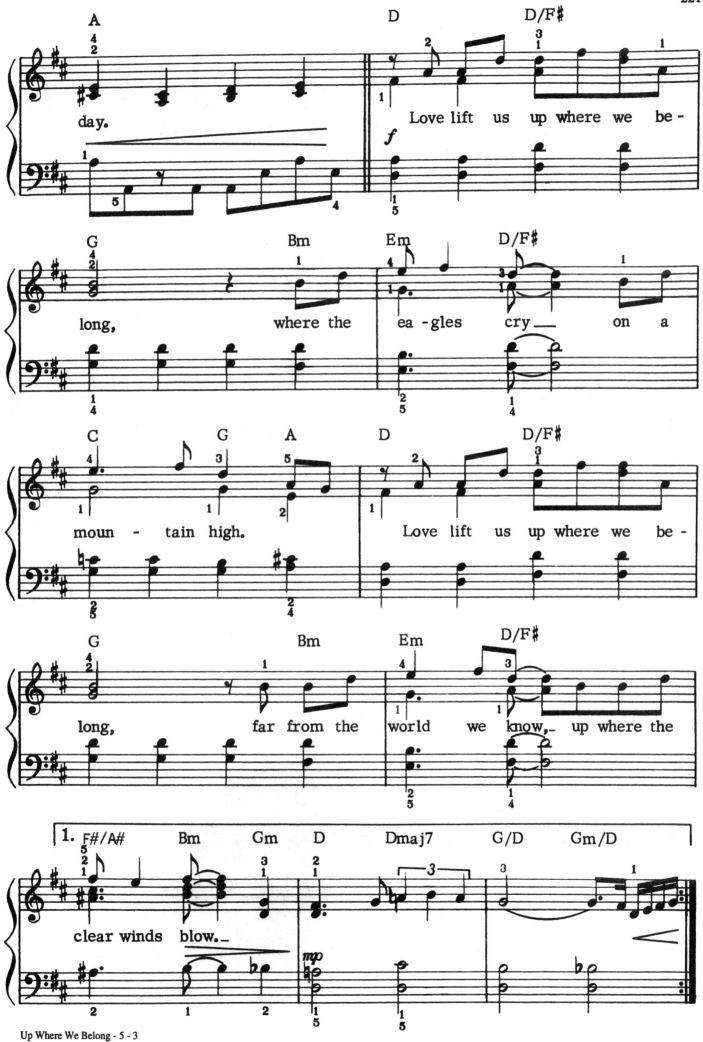

222

Additional Lyrics

2. Some hang on to "used-to-be",
   Live their lives looking behind.
   All we have is here and now;
   All our life, out there to find.
   The road is long.
   There are mountains in our way,
   But we climb them a step every day.

SEND IN THE CLOWNS
(From "A Little Night Music")

Music and Lyrics by
STEPHEN SONDHEIM
Arranged by DAN COATES

Slowly, with expression

226

OVER THE RAINBOW

Words by
E. Y. HARBURG

Music by
HAROLD ARLEN
Arranged by DAN COATES

Columbia Pictures Presents a New Vision Production "WHITE NIGHTS"

SEPARATE LIVES
(Love Theme from "White Nights")

Words and Music by
STEPHEN BISHOP
Arranged by DAN COATES

Freely, with expression

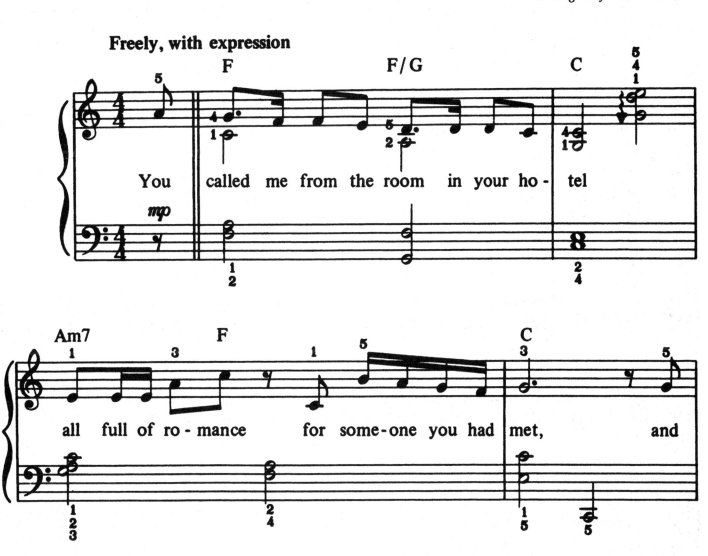

You called me from the room in your ho- tel all full of ro- mance for some-one you had met, and

tell- ing me how sor-ry you were leav-ing so soon, and that you

Separate Lives - 5 - 1

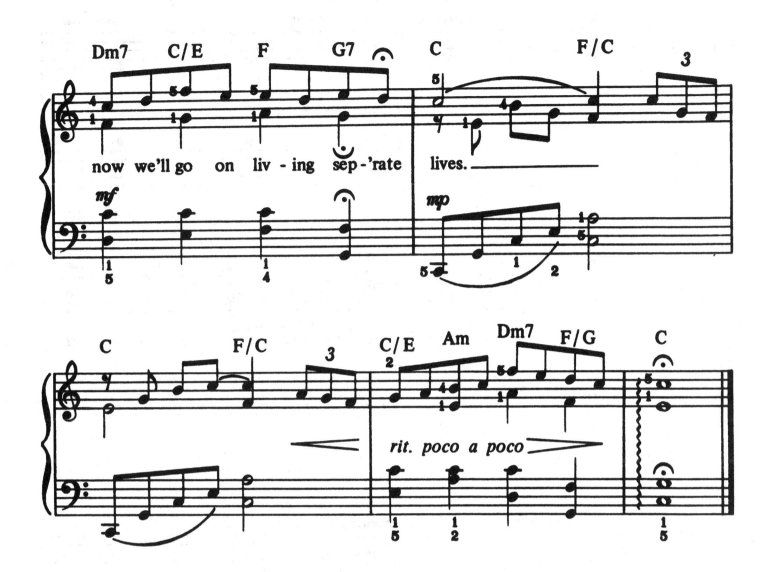

now we'll go on liv - ing sep -'rate lives.

Chorus 2:

Well, I held on to let you go.
And if you lost your love for me,
You never let it show.
There was no way to compromise.
So now we're living separate lives.

Chorus 3:

You have no right to ask me how I feel.
You have no right to speak to me so kind.
Someday I might find myself looking in your eyes.
But for now, we'll go on living separate lives.
Yes, for now we'll go on living separate lives.

Theme from
"LOVE AFFAIR"

Composed by
ENNIO MORRICONE
Arranged by DAN COATES

Gentle, flowing

(with pedal throughout)

Theme from "Love Affair" - 2 - 1

From the United Artists Motion Picture "NEW YORK, NEW YORK"

THEME FROM NEW YORK, NEW YORK

Words by
FRED EBB

Music by
JOHN KANDER
Arranged by DAN COATES

Theme from New York, New York - 5 - 1

Theme from New York, New York - 5 - 4

Theme from New York, New York - 5 - 5

From the Motion Picture "ANNIE"

TOMORROW

Lyrics by
MARTIN CHARNIN

Music by
CHARLES STROUSE
Arranged by DAN COATES

Tomorrow - 3 - 1

From the Motion Picture Soundtrack "BUSTER"

TWO HEARTS

Words by
PHIL COLLINS

Music by
LAMONT DOZIER
Arranged by DAN COATES

Two Hearts - 5 - 1

Extra Lyrics:

Well there's no easy way to, to understand it
There's so much of my life in her
And it's like I planned it
And it teaches you to never let go
There's so much love you'll never know
She can reach you no matter how far
Wherever you are.

(Chorus:)

LANE'S THEME

Composed by
BILL CONTI
Arranged by DAN COATES

Lane's Theme - 3 - 2

Lane's Theme - 3 - 3

From the Original Motion Picture Soundtrack "FREE WILLY"

WILL YOU BE THERE
(Theme from "Free Willy")

Written and Composed by
MICHAEL JACKSON
Arranged by DAN COATES

Moderate Gospel Feel

Hold me____ like the Riv - er Jor - dan, and I will then
wear - y____ tell me will you hold me, when wrong, will you

say to thee you are my friend.____
scold me, when lost will you find me? But they

Car - ry me, like you are my broth - er. Love me like a
told me a man should be faith - ful and walk when not

From the Vestron Motion Picture "DIRTY DANCING"

(I'VE HAD) THE TIME OF MY LIFE

Words and Music by
FRANKE PREVITE, DONALD MARKOWITZ
and JOHN DeNICOLA
Arranged by DAN COATES

(I've Had) The Time of My Life - 4 - 1

Verse 2:
With my body and soul
I want you more than you'll ever know.
So we'll just let it go,
Don't be afraid to lose control.
Yes, I know what's on your mind
When you say, "Stay with me tonight."
Just remember: You're the one thing
I can't get enough of,
So I'll tell you something,
This could be love. Because...
Chorus:
I've had the time of my life,
And I've searched through every open door
Till I've found the truth,
And I owe it all to you.

Theme from the Motion Picture "WITH HONORS"
I'LL REMEMBER

Written by
PATRICK LEONARD,
MADONNA CICCONE and
RICHARD PAGE
Arranged by DAN COATES

Moderately slow

I'll Remember - 4 - 1

264

I'll Remember - 4 - 3

D.S. 𝄋 al Coda ⊕

I'll Remember - 4 - 4

PACHELBEL CANON IN D

By
JOHANN PACHELBEL
Arranged by DAN COATES

Pachelbel Canon in D - 4 - 2

Pachelbel Canon in D - 4 - 3

Pachelbel Canon in D - 4 - 4

Featured in the M-G-M Picture "THE WIZARD OF OZ"

WE'RE OFF TO SEE THE WIZARD
(The Wonderful Wizard of Oz)

Lyric by
E.Y. HARBURG

Music by
HAROLD ARLEN
Arranged by DAN COATES

Moderate march tempo

Fol-low the yel-low brick road, fol-low the yel-low brick road.

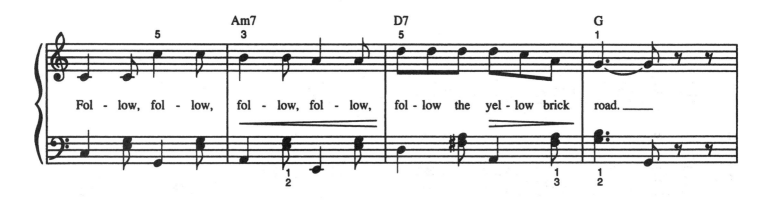

Fol-low, fol-low, fol-low, fol-low, fol-low the yel-low brick road.____

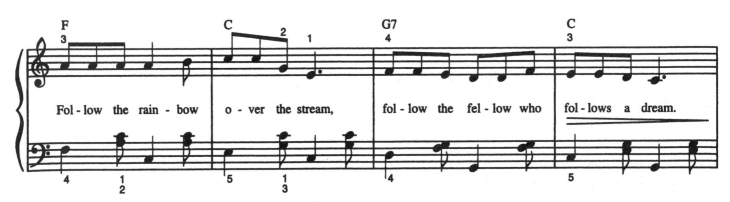

Fol-low the rain-bow o-ver the stream, fol-low the fel-low who fol-lows a dream.

We're Off to See the Wizard - 3 - 1

We're Off to See the Wizard - 3 - 2

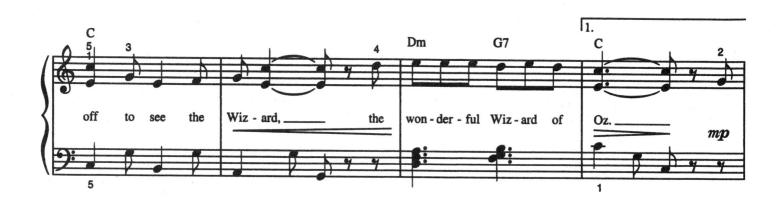

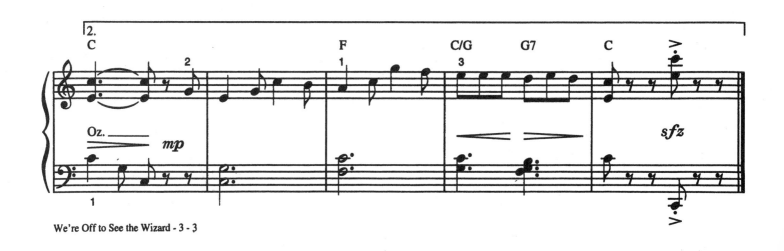

We're Off to See the Wizard - 3 - 3